Tails'

Tales

BY MIKE PEARCE

DEDICATION

This book is dedicated to animal enthusiasts and all those interested in knowing more about tails and the use of this word in our daily lives.

CONTENTS

ACKNOWLEDGMENTS

Christine Pearce for support in checking the manuscript

1 WHAT IS A TAIL?

The origin of the word tail comes from old English taegl. This is linked to the Old Norse word tagl meaning a horses tail. In Gothic tagl means hair or the twisted whip end of a rope.

How did tails come about? Bilateral symmetry (the same on each side) may have evolved in young forms of sea animals, which unlike tunicates today, swam in the seas but did not settle down as adults. They had a tail and a primitive nerve chord which was not lost as in tunicates when they settle on the sea floor.

The word tail often relates to the end and something long and bendy long. It can also be used to represent numerous objects such as a stream of smoke, the length of hair or even a long queue of people and can move. In vertebrates it exists if present, at the base of the vertebral column and can acts as an extra limb. In humans the coccyx is a vestigial tail and is formed from three to five vertebrae and is joined to the sacrum. Even if not extended as a true tail it forms a site for muscle attachment which is important for supporting your weight when sitting.

Animals which have a tail can have as many as forty seven vertebrae, as in the pangolin vertebrae the pangolin reaching as many as forty seven. This is small compared to diplodocus a dinosaur which had an extremely long tail with around eighty vertebrae, twice as many as some of the other dinosaurs. The size of each vertebra decreases as you move towards the end of the tail and the muscles, tendons and nerves become smaller, making it more flexible.

2 FORM AND FUNCTION OF TAILS IN ANIMALS

For animals without legs the tail has been used for movement, especially in water. Water, especially salt water, is denser than air so tails can be used to help propel these creatures along whether they are a ribbon like feature on the top of the tail or a flattened end.

Bait or prey sweepers

Some animals may use their tails to lure animals closer so that they can capture them. An example is the spider tailed snake of the North Arabian Desert. At the end of its tail it has a growth which looks like a spider. This can attract birds, reptiles and small mammals that think it is a camel spider. Mexican cantil vipers and some other snakes also move their tails like wriggling worms and often have brightly coloured tips to attract prey. The spiny lizard also can shake its tail when trying to capture food. Thresher sharks can use their tails to stun fish with one blow and then eat them. Crocodiles also can herd shoals of fish towards the banks with their tails.

Balance

A lot of animals use their tails for balance when moving especially if they move fast.

Some dinosaurs may have used their tails in this way just as lions, tigers, dogs and cats do so today. This use of tails at speed helps them with sudden turns. Balance is also important for momentum as seen in kangaroos and jerboa while jumping. Road running tails help them with balance when they swing from side to side. Pine martins, flying squirrels and lemurs' tails help with balance when jumping from tree to tree. In fennec foxes the tail helps them change direction when running.

The tail is also useful for balance when running along narrow objects Examples of this are rats running along thin ropes or chains, and cats running along fence tops. Birds in flight can also use tails for balance to give lift or furl them, especially at high speeds.

Chasing

Young animals, such as lions and cats, often chase and pounce on their playmates' tails. This is good practice for learning how to suddenly pounce on their prey when they become adult. Some dogs, such as German shepherds and terriers especially, like to chase their tails. They can chase their tails clockwise or anticlockwise, and this is often seen as puppies and they grow out of it. Chasing may be just for play but can indicate an obsession, boredom or even a medical problem at the hind end. Grabbing animals such as mice by the tail can also help prevent them from biting you.

Communication

Communication by tail can be by its appearance, movement, scent wafting or sound they make. Ring tails are common. Greater than half of the order of carnivores - tigers, leopards, cheetahs etc. have tails with different coloured rings. These can be used to indicate danger or to keep a group of animals together.

The interpretation of behaviour from tail wagging is widespread. A lot of studies have been made to suggest what these actually mean. Some dogs' tails were originally used for balance but became adapted for signaling, especially when they became domesticated. . Tails can be higher up in the spine in dogs such as terriers and beagles (the scent hounds), but placed lower in dogs such as greyhounds and Afghans. If dogs only have small tails, or are docked so that their moods cannot be seen then they tend to be more cautious with other dogs. If dogs wag their tails to the left this may mean they are threatened in some way. But wagging to the right can mean they have found something pleasant, such as a bone.

Holding a tail high can be a sign of dominance and authority and a way of releasing more pheromones from their two scent glands under their tail. If, at the same time, the tail is wagging this means they are also happy and excited. However if the tail is totally upright it can mean a dog is on guard or ready to chase. This is seen in game dogs when they spot a prey and want to indicate this to their owner. Dogs with a small curly tail will also increase the tightness if alert. If the tail is held horizontally to the ground then the dog may be interested in something and is sniffing. With slow wagging and the tail held low then the dog is worrying or not sure about something. If the tail drops further and is tucked between its legs it feels threatened and is submitting. A tail between the legs also means that less scent is given off so this deters other dogs from sniffing and trying to mate.

Cats' tails also give some indications of mood. They are happy when their tails are held up high and even happier if tails are quivering at the end. If they swing their tails back and forth then they are annoyed, and if their tails are straight out and they are crouching and twitching they are excited and ready to attack. Whilst sleeping their tails can curl around them.

Other animals may indicate moods with their tails. Cattle and deer can raise their tails if curious and raise them even higher as a warning. Squirrels can shake their tails if upset or frightened or use their tail as a signal in a whipping movement. Giraffes are also believed to communicate using their tails and gophers use their tails to help find their way in dark tunnels. In lizards the bearded dragons tail twitches and may be raised when stressed or hunting. It also twitches at breeding and is raised when it is appears happy.

In the sea, tail flukes of whales or dolphins can hit the water with great force so as to send a message to others. Beavers also use their flat tail to hit water or logs to send messages. The sound can also ward off moose, which eat their young shoots on branches they collected. It has been suggested that peacocks, when shaking their tails produce, a low frequency sound which can be picked up by others. The male racquet bird has, at the end of it tail, feathers which look like a tennis racquet. This, it flicks up and down, to give a whip - like sound. Also Wilson's snipes' tail feathers click during courtship. Hippos, by moving their tails in the water, help to distribute their faeces which sends messages to others.

Snails and slugs have extensions of their muscular foot which are often referred to as tails. These help lay the slime trails and with direction. The slug <u>Derocerus</u> also produces attractants and can even wave its tail for other slugs to follow. Bristle tails have central long cerci. Mayflies have three long tails, stoneflies two. Earwigs have forceps at their ends and scorpion flies have swollen genitalia. Leeches have suckers on their tail and flukes and flatworms and tapeworms have tail like movements of their bodies.

Courtship and display

For humans women tend to put on a display to attract the opposite sex. This is the reverse in many animals, especially birds, whose elaborate displays and actions involving their tail feathers are used to attract a mate. The peacock is a familiar example with a huge fan of tail feathers containing rows of distinct eye like patterns down their length. Charles Darwin could not see why evolution had resulted in peacocks sacrificing their safety to exhibit this display. He said "while I gaze at a peacock's tail it makes me sick"!

Some dinosaurs are believed to have shaken their fan like feathers to attract mates. Bird tail feathers, as with peacocks, can reach huge sizes and be very colourful. New Guinea and northern Australia have many birds of paradise with beautiful coloured plumage and tail feathers.

The lyre tailed night jar has a tail eight times as long as its body. Lyre birds can put their two lyre shaped feathers over their bodies during courtship. The New Guinea ribbon tail bird can have a tail over three feet long. The red bird of paradise has two wiry tail feathers and the blue birds of paradise can hang upside down and rotate, spreading out their plumose tails and vibrate their whole bodies. King birds of paradise have two long thin tail feathers with racquets. The Quetzal has long tailed coverts which extend beyond their tail like a wedding train. Scissor tail flycatcher feathers stream behind it and does acrobatics in the air. Game birds also .can have spectacular tails Jungle fowl have plumes and pheasants have a long tail. Also male turkeys can open up their tail feathers to attract females

Defence

Some dinosaurs had armoured tails or defensive clubs at the end of the tail. Some, like <u>Stegosaurus</u> and <u>Shunosaurus</u>, had tail spikes at the end of the tail. Huge bony flattened clubs were seen in some dinosaurs such as <u>Ankylosaurus</u> which they swung out using their hips for combat. **Long thin tails in dinosaurs may also have acted like whips which made a warning noise to deter predators.**

Chameleons can coil up their tails and release these when predators approach. Armadillos are also able to roll up their tails within their bodies for defence. Moths and some butterflies have extensions of their wings which can be considered tails. The slipper moth has two tails, and the blue hairstreak has two tails on either side. Some uraniid moths have three tail extensions on each side of the wing.

The scissor tail bird has a tail which can be twice the length of the body and this makes a hissing sound when flying which may put off predators.

One common form of defence is to attract predators towards their tails rather than their body or head. Many reptiles can vibrate their tails if disturbed. The rattlesnake has a ten segmented rattle. A horny section of its tail is loosely connected so as to give the rattle sound when shaken. Some snakes have brightly coloured tips on their tails and flattened ends which they wave in the air to mimic heads. If attacked, the rubber boa puts its head in its coils and its tail in the air so there is less damage. Burrowing snakes, like the three lined snake from Trinidad, may have a sharp pointed scale on the end of their tails which can pierce the skin when handled making you think you have been bitten. Side winder snakes also have a rattle and are able to throw their bodies onto the sand so as to move diagonally.

Some snakes can also detect infra-red rays emitted from prey. Ground squirrels have found a way to change their focus the infra-red detection to their tails pumping extra warm blood into the tail so that the snakes only concentrate on the infra-red glow stick of their tail so that they can escape. This flagging method of escape is also made use of by rabbits which can confuse their predators by flashing the white underside of their small bobtail. This confuses the predator making it possible to escape. A similar thing is seen in deer but this may also be a signal to keep the herd together. In winter weasels can turn white but their tail tip may remain black. This also acts as a decoy for predators to attack instead of the head and body allowing better escape.

Lizards are able to lose their tails if attacked. These tails can remain wriggling on the ground attracting the predator

The northern leaf tailed gecko has a flattened tail which looks exactly like a leaf giving camouflage. It also can lose its tail if attacked. The armadillo lizard has spines on its body and tail. It grasps its tail in its mouth to form a ring so it is protected.

Many fish have large eyespots near the end of their tails so that they are not attacked from the front. They may even have a dark stripe across their eyes to help conceal them.

Some animals, such as skunks, will raise their tails to give off a blast of scent as a warning. The ring tailed lemur has stink fights pushing out scent from its glands onto its tail; it rubs this on its wrists and also flicks its tail at other males.

Animals may also raise their tails over their bodies so as to look bigger. Ferrets, like cats, can bush up their tails to make them bigger, especially if frightened or in conflict. Some others, such as scorpions, have a sting at the end of their tail. Vinegaroons (whip scorpions) have a long telson which is a sensory organ and have glands at the end of their abdomen which can spray acetic acid (vinegar).

Digging

Tails can be used for digging. The spiked shaped tail telson of the horseshoe crab is used for digging in sand. It also helps it to upright itself if turned over. The platypus tail can push loose earth out of the way when digging.

Food storage

This is common in large tails. Gila monsters have rounded large tails which act as reservoirs for fat during hibernation Alligators also use tails to store fat and even the duck billed platypus, with beaver like tails use them for the same purpose. Many large cattle also have large stores of fat in their tails. The platypus stores 50% of its body fat in its tail.

Grasping (prehensile tails)

Animals that live in trees often have prehensile tails to prevent them from falling or to help with movement. Snakes can be thought of as a very long tail with a head. Boas and some other snakes can coil round branches for support. Others which coil around are seahorses which hold onto weed as an anchor to stop them being swept away by currents. Some often have protrusions on their body and tail to match the weed.

Some mice, such as harvest mice, will coil their tails around corn stalks while eating the corn heads. The prehensile tail is very common in new world monkeys and opossums. Spider monkeys in tropical rain forests of South and Central America use their tails like another limb to get them from tree to tree across long distances in search for fruit. The grey wooly monkey has a gripping pad on the underside of the rear tail top. Opossums have a hairless tail. The babies will cling to this tail on their mothers' backs until they can support their whole weight by their own tails. Raccoons and its relations also use their tails when climbing trees. The bushy tail of the ring-tailed glider helps it to grasp branches to help it in its flight from tree to tree.

Holding

Elephants especially young ones' hold each other's tails when moving in a line across country to keep them together. Tails can also get tangled together, an example being rats when populations become very high. A rat king is where at birth a number of tails get tangled together and become fixed with excrement and dirt. Over thirty tails can be tangled together and inseparable. The babies develop together but their tails are damaged.

Lashing

Dinosaurs, for defence, could lash their tails in a similar way that crocodiles and alligators do today. In water this helps for propulsion when they spin around when feeding. The kangaroo tail is used for lashing at enemies.

For defence it lashes at enemies. The Komodo dragon tail is used as a weapon and for support if standing on hind legs. The thorny devil lizard and horned lizard have thorn- like spines on their tails. Sting rays can lash their tails at enemies and the spines at the base of their tail contain poison.

Propulsion and steering and brakes

Propulsion and steering by tails reaches a wide spectrum in the water where tails may be adapted for manoeuvrability and speed. This is seen especially in fish where tails, by moving side to side, propel the fish forward and also act as a rudder to steer them in the right direction.

There are many different shapes of tails. Fan shaped tails are good for short burst of speed, especially for those living on the sea floor. If the tail is rounded at the back it can have good front acceleration but has a lot of drag expending a lot of energy when it is used. If the tail is straight at the back, this can reduce the drag slightly. A swallow's tail, if forked reduces drag while still giving good manoeuvrability and speed. Further forking will increase acceleration, especially if stiffer, but this affects manoeuvrability as seen in great white sharks. The indentation is crescent shape in some of the fastest fish e.g. swordfish.

If the upper part of the fork is bigger than the lower fork, as in the thresher or tiger shark, this helps them swim downwards. They can even stun fish with this part of the tail. The upper part can also be more expanded with a blunt end as in the nurse shark or cookie cutter. This is good for sudden bursts of acceleration. Early lizards may also have had shark like tails. The fin can run along the body to the tail this is seen in some eels. This helps them move into small cracks or tight spaces between rocks. Fish can also have single fin like paddles or a very elongated flattened tail such as lung fish. Flying fish jump out of water and while gliding beat their tails to gain height.

Flat horizontal tails are seen in bottom feeders which give them some lift as seen in flounders, halibut and turbot. Muskrats and duck billed platypus and beavers also have horizontal tails which form the same function. Lobsters and shrimps also have flattened horizontal tails which they flick at intervals to move them forward.

Whales and dolphins have fibrous forked tails with no bones or muscles which help them move up and down in water. The dugong has a crescent shaped tail. Ichthyosaurs had powerful tails for fast propulsion and <u>Mosaurus</u> and <u>Tylosaurus</u> shot through the sea with thrashing tails. Some reptiles too have strong tails for propulsion in water, such as crocodiles, sea lizards and marine iguanas in the Galapagos. Their tails help them when swimming, acting as a rudder. Kuhl's flying geckos have fringes on their tails which help control flight.

Propulsion is seen in primitive organisms. Bacteria can use flagella which can rotate like helicopter blades for propulsion. Some also move in a corkscrew movement, for example, spirillum. Flagellate single celled animals (protozoa) can use their flagella in a whip like fashion in water to propel them or in the gut fluids as seen in the parasitic flagellate Giardia. Even the human sperm cell has a tail like flagellum for propulsion.

Tails in birds can affect speed and drag just like fish. Examples of tails include rounded forked, fan shaped, notched, square, plus other forms. In slow flight birds can spread out their tail feathers and lower them down at various angles. If they speed up it reduces the angle and high speeds may curl its tail feathers in. On landing, tail feathers are put upwards. In thermals the tail can be tilted in different directions to the angle of attack. The tail feathers in birds can have an important role in braking and steering. By spreading out their tail feathers, especially if long, birds such as the skua and birds of prey can steer at low speeds, hover and glide. Tails also act as a rudder in fast flying. Even the dinosaurs <u>Microraptor</u> and <u>Oviraptor</u> had diamond shaped tail fans which may have acted as a break or rudder.

Bushy tails help those animals which move in the trees such as flying squirrels. Some flying lemurs have membrane attached to their tails and squirrel gliders use their tails as a rudder when parachuting. Many bats have their tails joined to their membranous wings. Geckos, if they fall off objects or walls, will rotate their tails to ensure they land on their feet.

Running animals such as cheetahs may use tails as a rudder when chasing prey which help them change direction. The position of the tail can vary for different animals when running. The cote runs with its tail down, dogs with their tails up and wolves with their tails straight-out. Lizards when moving can often hold their tails out straight and stiff. In water thick or flattened tails can help them steer. This is seen in beavers and some of the breeds of dogs.

<u>Support</u>

In dinosaurs, especially the plant eaters like
<u>Bronchiosaurus</u>, the tail may have served as a
counterbalance for the very long neck. The middle
part of the tail had extra bones on the underside,
which gave <u>Diplodocus </u>its name. Dinosaurs on two
legs, such as tyrannosaurus and <u>Gigantosaurus</u>, would
use their tails as a prop. Even today some animals like
kangaroos have long strong tails which act as a tripod
with the hind legs and are used for support when
sitting upright. This mean they can reach food easier
as well as use their hind and front limbs for defence.
The Komodo dragon also uses its tail in this way for
support when standing on its hind leg, and even
beavers prop themselves up on their wide tails in the
same way so as to chew logs.

Bird's tails have a bony support surrounded by
muscle to which is attached tail feathers. These
feathers in some birds such as woodpeckers may be
stiff and strong and can help support them especially

if clinging onto the side of tree trunks. Cobras can coil their tails to support the rest of their body.

Swatters

Grazing animals often flick their tails to help remove insects which are attracted to their hind ends. The tails often have large strands of hair at the end. The giraffe tail is short with a flattened hairy end. The camel's tail is shorter, flattened but possibly not as good a fly swatter but it does have a good tuft of hair at its end The Zebra has a flair of black hair up to fifty six centimeters long which is used to swat flies. The tail of the Rhino is a bit longer but not much good as it is just skin

Temperature control and for warmth

The tail of the rat, as with other hairless tails, may act as heat exchange organs where more blood can dilate the blood vessel in the tail so it loses losing heat. Many animals have bushy tails which can help them to keep warm, especially during the winter or hibernation. The tail often covers their nose to prevent heat loss. Examples include foxes, squirrels, dogs, wolves, cats and anteaters. Arctic or Nordic breeds of dogs have double layers of fur on their body and tails to protect them in cold climates. They can pull their tails over their faces to keep out the cold. Some species of bat have a thick layer of fur on their tail membranes for insulation when roosting. The platypus is able to curl its tail against its chest so as to help incubate its eggs

<u>Whips</u>

Dinosaurs such as brachiosaurus may have used tails as whips which became more lethal if they were covered in spines. Green iguanas and whip tailed lizards are examples of whips in reptiles

3 TAIL LOSS, SMALL TAILS OR NO TAILS

If lizards as well as some other reptiles like geckos, skinks, salamanders and glass snakes, are held or they become stressed or attacked they will break their tails bones or break the section between vertebrae and their tails will fall off. The tail is left wriggling on the ground which confuses the predator. In some skinks it is also brightly coloured unlike the rest of the body so gives an added attraction. In lizards the tail never grows the same and it is supported by cartilage not bone. There are no limits to losses. Broken ends will heal rapidly but may be shorter than the original tail. There may be two or even three new tails but they can be different lengths. A black and white tegu lizard with a partially severed tail grew six new tails. Slow worms lose tails but they are slow to grow. One can also breed animals with several tails e.g. the fantail goldfish

Amphibians, (frogs and toads) as tadpoles lose their tails which are reabsorbed by sixteen weeks. Squirrels can also lose tails to escape predators as told in stories such as Beatrix Potter is Squirrel Nutkin.

Humans have a tail as embryos. The gene Wnt-3a is believed responsible and is switched off possibly originally by a mutation. It has been suggested that tails were lost due to emphasis on the use of hands and feet. However, two kinds of tails are sometimes found in humans. The first is a soft tail with no bones but nerves and voluntary muscles, fat and connective tissue. These can reach as much as thirteen centimetres in length.

Similar tails but with bones, often five, can be found as well. These are common in those with spina bifida where the vertebrae are not properly formed and the tail can extend as a growing sac. This tail can move. An example of this was seen in India in 2002 where a boy had a bony tail which reached ten centimetre but was not active, as it had no nerve chord. An American surgeon is prepared to transplant tails onto

humans and there is a lot of interest in this. Old
world primates such as chimps, gorillas and
orangutans also do not have tails. Barbary apes have
small tails with no vertebrae. Human sperm often
contains many that have no tails or many tails but this
affects their swimming.

Guinea pigs and capybara also do not have tails. The
Manx cat does not have a tail which is attributed to its
tail being shut in the door of Noah's ark before it
sailed away. There is a saying if you pick up a guinea
pig by the tail its eyes will fall out but the tail is so
short it would be hard to hold it. Rabbits have a bob
tail and hamsters have reduced tails. Many animals
can be bred with no tails such as mice and chickens.
Bats have their tails incorporated into their wings; the
flying fox has no tail though.

There is a whole variety of tails found in dogs. The
normal original dog had lots of hair like a wolf. .
Bulldogs have a twisted tight corkscrew or curled tail
and tufted tails at the end are found in poodles.
Others include, flag pole tails upright as in beagles,

saber shaped tails as in German shepherds, sword tails as in corgis, carrot shaped tails as in terriers and rattail as in the nearly hairless Afghans. Cold weather dogs tend to have sickle shaped tails which are curved frontwards. Long tails with thick fur are good for swimming as in Labradors and called the otter tail in retrievers. Natural bob tails can be found in King Charles spaniels, Jack Russell terriers, and Pembroke welsh corgis. Bob tails are found in rabbits and deer but also found in some cats (American or Japanese bobtails). Cats can also have corkscrew or curly tails. The Siamese cat often has a kink in its tail but this is only found when you feel it. This is believed to be because it remained curved after it let a princess store her rings on it. Hen's eggs in China have been laid with tails as long as three centimetres hanging outside. Mutations can sometimes produce more than one tail in cats.

Many tails can be docked in animals but in some countries this is restricted, especially in dogs. Dogs without tails can lose their ability to communicate with each other if tails are docked. Lambs have their tails docked, which protects their anus from being covered in faeces which could attract wool maggots. Some sheep such as those from Scandinavia and Northern Europe have short tails and don't need to be docked. These are rat tailed sheep. Cows' tails also used to be docked to prevent infections. Pigs' curly tails are often docked so that other pigs don't bite them so as to cause infections. Some horses such as those pulling vehicles are also docked to prevent tangling. In the New Forest horses can have their tails cut in different ways when rounded up to represent what area of the forest they came from.

4 OTHER TAILS

Bible

There are several references to tails in the Bible:

Exodus 4:4 the Lord tells Moses to hold the snake by the tail which becomes a staff. Exodus 29:22 and Leviticus 3:9, 7:3, 8:25, 9:19 all refer to taking fat from the fatty tail of the ram and fat from other body parts. Fat tailed sheep with fat in the tail and rump are common in Africa, Middle East and Asia and have been introduced to the US.

Deuteronomy 28:13 the Lord refers to Moses and the Israelites as the head and not the tail if they listen to the commandments. Meshach and Abednego were to be made the head not the tail by God.

Isaiah 9:14 refers to the head and tail of Israel and 9:14 refers to the head being the elder and honourable man, and the prophet who teaches the falsehood is the tail.

Judges 15:4 states how Samson caught three hundred foxes and put them tail to tail. He then lit a torch in the middle.

Revelation 9:10 mentions Abaddon, or the destroyer, the angel of the bottomless pit. There are horse like locusts with scorpion tails which sting their victims. They have long hair and wear crowns and armour and hurt men for five months.

Revelation 9:19 also refers to horses having tails.12:4 refers to how the dragon's tail swept away a third of the stars of heaven and threw them to the earth. The dragon then stood before the woman who was about to give birth so that when she gave birth he might devour her.

<u>Bounty</u>

Where overpopulation of nuisance species occurs then the public are asked to help reduce numbers and rewarded. Often the presentation of tails for money occurs.

Bounties for animals have been going on for thousands of years. The Romans tried this for a mouse plague in Spain. Also in medieval times bounties occurred.

A reward for rat tails was given in French colonial times in Vietnam. However, people would cut off the rats' tails and then release them to breed more in the sewer. Also this encourages people to breed more animals themselves so as to produce more available tails, an example being in Georgia for pigs' tails.

In 1932 the forestry Commission would give 2.5p per tail. In 1943 as many as 3630 tails were collected in a month and there was a constant stream of small boys and old men demanding their money. Tails even arrived in parcels in the post. In the 1950s in UK the Ministry of Agriculture reintroduced this and gave sixpence for tails of grey squirrels as they had become a pest species.

In the 60s it was reported that some landowners would consider cash returns for tails or other body parts of sparrows crows, wood pigeons and squirrels. The government stated that little good was done by the bounty on grey squirrels and over five years £80,000 had been paid out.

In 1999 a trust in Anglesey, North Wales put a bounty of £1 for squirrels so as to protect red squirrel populations. In 2004 the liberal democrats again suggested a bounty for grey squirrels as they were destroying trees, eating birds' eggs and had transmitted rabies to a human through a bite.

In 2014 the government in Louisiana placed a bounty on swamp rat tails (Nutria) which were breeding at high rates and even alligators could not keep populations down. Tails had to be presented longer than seven inches and be fresh or kept in ice. In New Mexico gophers' tails have a bounty and tails had to be handed in on a certain day.

Philippine farmers in 2105, suffering the effects of El Nino have been given rice for rat tails as they will damage crops.

<u>Business</u>

Fat tail and long tailed probability analysis is used in financial risk management. The tail starts away from the mean. A fat-tailed distribution is one of the so-called heavy-tailed statistical distributions that describe the probability of certain events. Fat tails have a sharp bell shape. A probability distribution can show that moderately extreme outcomes were more likely than expected. A long tailed distribution is one in which very extreme outcomes should not be ignored. The main markets are the head and the economy is now moving to a larger number of niches (the tail). A thick tail expression is used in to judge values at risk evaluation.

Cat o'nine tails

This consisted of nine leather or rope cords or tails that represent the nine lives of a cat. The whip also made marks like the scratches of a cat. On board ship this whip was kept in a bag, and this led to the expression the 'cat was let out of the bag'. It was used for flogging of military personnel up to the nineteenth century. The Egyptians believed that when beaten with cat hide, the victim gained virtue from the whip.

Tail Coats

A tailcoat has the front cut away leaving the rear part which is called tails. This was to make it easier when riding a horse. You can have a morning or evening tail coat

Morning coat has a split at back so it sits over the back of the horse. It became a standard part of clothing for upper classes in the late 19th century to be worn before noon. The same coat was then worn in evenings and then called a cutaway

After the war, the morning coat slowly fell out of fashion and today only members of the upper classes or a groom at a wedding continue to wear this elegant garment.

Cocktails

The cocktail was derived from the early 17th century: from cock plus tail.. It originally described an animal with the tail of a cock. The earliest known use for a drink was in 1806 but it is also found in a Vermont newspaper from 1803. Cocktails are mixed drinks using spirits mixed with other ingredients

DNA

To get the whole of the DNA spiral in a cell it is tightly packed by wrapping around ball like histone proteins which have flexible tails of amino acids used to link the strands.

Food

Tails were an important cheap food source in the past for some people but are still used today in some countries. Some animals such as lizards, when they lose their tails, may eat them. Lambs' tails pie was popular in Kent and needed twenty- four tails to produce it.

Today tails from cattle and relatives are a common source of food. Oxtail from ox or even bison provides large portions. Slow cooking removes the meat which falls off. These tails are often very fatty and commonly used for stocks and soups. The narrow end of the fillet is often used for flash frying. Pigs tails can be smoked, roasted or salted and again may be used in stock and flavouring. They may even be roasted where the tail is split down one side, bones taken out to halfway and the tail boiled in water for an hour. They then are fired until crispy and can be served with a damson or other fruit sauce. Pigs' tails are also used with brains, skin trotters and tongue to make braun.

Alligator tail is a favourite in the United States and crocodile tail in South Africa Kangaroo tail in Australia is great in stews and soups and was often eaten by Aborigines. Catholics in the middle ages were allowed to eat beavers tails on fast days as they were considered fish and not animal.

Another famous tail used for soup is shark fin which is used for special occasions. Owing to the belief that the tails cure health problems this has led to depletion of sharks in some areas. It is said not to taste of much without flavourings.

Turkey tails are found in some markets in Ghana even though their sale is not allowed.Smoked turkey tails also exist in other countries. The tail end of a turkey or chicken is commonly known as the parson's nose and is very fatty and a delicacy in some parts of Japan. Other turkey tails are the bracket fungi which have concentric multicoloured rings like the tail of a turkey. These have been used for medicinal tea in China for many years.Lobster tails are now at a low price and are a delicacy especially when served with butter and lemon.Scorpion tails can be crushed along with some drugs and tobacco in Afghanistan to produce an intoxicant when smoked.

There is also yellow tail wine and Australian wine. This had tannins and acidity removed which people do not like. It has a bright yellow label with the picture of a wallaby in the centre.

<u>Fishing</u>

Fishing flies have to be identical to the tails they are mimicking. Dry flies have a long stiff tail with often iridescent materials incorporated. For making flies it is important to get big hollow hairs which have short tips and are usually lighter. Squirrel tails are good as they will ripple in the water

Pheasant tail nymphs are used for trout and grayling. Streamers for trout use black hair which is skinny like a worm and can have tinsel attached. Rubber mice tails are good as they fall into the water.

To pull out lug worms when the tail is exposed, the hand is used to dig it out and it is pulled out by the tail.

Fly Whisks

. In Africa these may be prized for use by humans as fly swatters and animals can be killed it is said for this. Yaks' tails are also used in the same way. Zulu fortune tellers can use these swatters to swat dark spirits which may interfere with their messages.

Insurance

This is where you can purchase extended coverage to ensure coverage if your insurance policy for medical or legal malpractices runs out.

Hair styles.

A long thin tail of hair once quite popular in the 1980s, growing down from the back of the hair is called the rattail. It can be different lengths and may be straightened or braided. Some people can have several of these and these are portrayed in many fictional characters such as Manga. Rattails are popular in Australia and parts of New Zealand. Often pirates in pictures and films are seen with these. The footballer, Cristiano Ronaldo, had one of these once. Rihanna modified this to produce a 'sting ray' tail.

Pigtails originate from the way they twisted chewing tobacco which they to hang up for drying which looked like a twisted pig's tail. They also fall down the back singly or one on each side. They can be braided or without braiding, may be referred to as a brunch or plaits if either side, or a ponytail if only a central, single brunch. Pigtails were at one time a fashion for military personnel and remain today in the wigs worn by barristers. In China two pigtails meant the girl was single while one indicated she was married. A Chinese man's hair piece the 'queue' is not termed a pigtail. Some pigtails can have beads or ribbons in them

The mermaid tail braid is a style for long hair where the hair at the back is divided into two and one piece tied up. The other piece is then divided into three pieces and an inverted braid carried out and tied off. The first piece is like the other piece divided into three and braided. Lose strands are tugged at and pulled out partially along the lengths and the two braids tied together at the bottom. The whole looking like a mermaid's tail.

Different kinds of fishtail braided hair are common in fashion shows etc. It involves criss-crossing and can be as a plait or in a bun. It involves making 4-5 pony tails and pulling through braided sections then allowing them to fall together and tie. A topsy tail is a tool which can be used to form different kinds and positions of braids or pony tails

Horse's tails are often braided to prevent them getting dirty or entangling in carts or reins. A glue may be used but you must not braid the tails if wet. Fish tail types can be produced. You can even braid in extensions using other horse's hair. You can also have tail bags and tail wraps to protect these tails.

It is common for the theft of horse hair in some countries or use as false hair for extensions. Cowboy Roy Rogers had his horse Trigger's tail hacked off while he was sleeping in a trailer. It is even reported that witches have been supposed to be braiding horses' tails at certain times of the year in Sussex.

Hundreds of stolen tails of dogs and cats were found scattered around in Brazilian towns- the reason unknown.

One can buy genuine fur or fake fur tail key chains or pendant charms. Silver fox is an example. Raccoon, fox or squirrel tails have also been sold to put in hats or used as car ornaments.Fox tails are also sold as sex toys for adult fun. Japanese fashion has included the use of tails attached to bags or belts. These can be bright colours and worn at events or festivals. Wearing tails on the outside on the left meant that a girl is available but on the right she has been taken.

In the 16th century mink or ermine tails were worn around the neck so that the fleas could move and not bite the owner. Cow tails have been worn on upper arms and below the knees to give the appearance of more bulk to the body. Tail hairs from horses, elephants and giraffes can be made into necklaces and bracelets. Horse hair was used as fabric and it was the fashion to cut horse tails in the 1800's. Factories were set up to produce this fabric which was also used for mattresses and padding inside seats.

Key board

The apestaart sign in Dutch means a monkey's tail. This is because it looks as though its tail is coiling over the top of a monkey.

Mechanisation

In Japan an electronic tail has been developed which can be attached to people. Its movements will indicate the mood that the person is in i.e. it wags when you are happy. A New York firm has also produced a first emotion sensor for a dog's tail which can capture and analyse their movements. In the US a companion robotic cat has also been developed to keep the elderly company.

People and places

Thousands of people have the surname Tail. Other surnames containing tail are Wipetail and Taiilard. Spotted Tail was a Sioux leader. He was the nephew of Crazy Horse and was shot by Crow Dog after being accused of selling part of the reservation.

Marco Island. has a street named Tigertail. This originates from the nickname of a famous Florida Seminole Indian leader during the Second Seminole Indian War, Tigertail received his nickname from the U.S. army soldiers because he wore a long strip of panther skin hanging from his waist.

Red and White Tail Street is found in California, Wolftail in Canada. Beaver Tail road is in Minnesota. Fox Tail Drive can be found in York city.

Chicago Park district has Cotton Tailed Park called so because the park is filled with cotton-tailed rabbits that neighbourhood children love to chase.

.The Tail of the Dragon, is a portion of U.S. Route 129 in Blount County, Tennessee that looks like a dragon's tail. It has 318 curves in 11 miles. The sharpest blind curves have nicknames such as Wheelie Hell and there is a tree of shame on which pieces of crashed vehicles are hung.

Danelaw counties were those parts ruled by the Danes and the tail was a narrow strip of land.

The grey mare's tail is one of Scotland's finest waterfalls in the Moffat hills

Petticoat tails

A Petticoat Tail is the name given to triangular pieces of shortbread. This used to contain caraway seeds and was a favourite of Mary Queen of Scots. The origin is believed to be from ladies' petticoats of the 12th century, tally being the name for the pattern of cloth used.

Postage

The Otter Tail County Enhanced 911 addressing system was created to save lives during emergencies. This addressing system meets all postal requirements of the U.S. Postal Service, meaning people can be found quickly.

Sky

Clouds that look like mares' tails in the sky are caused by high cirrus clouds that have been shaped by the upper winds. Cirrus clouds can signal an approaching storm system.

Tail clouds are low- lying, tail -shaped clouds. These can extend from a thunderstorm to a wall cloud. Some of these clouds are caused by condensation trails in the sky from planes. These are more common in wet, cold air and can stay visible for long periods related to altitude after which they become more dispersed.

Comet trails consist of streams of dust and ionised gas which are made visible by the sun's rays. These tails point away from the sun but the gas tails can change direction caused by the solar winds. The Hubble space station has shown that asteroids can produce, at timed intervals, as many as six tails of dust radiating from it like spokes on a bike.

Kites have tails. If they had no tail, or a small tail they would spin around in the sky. The tail helps provide drag and weight. Drag can be reduced with a flatter tail. One can use longer tails but weight may be prohibitive. In the South Sea Islands the tails of kites have been used for fishing. The bait and a net are tied to the end. In China huge kites were used to transport men into the sky to spy and in the 19th century the tails were used to carry meteorological instruments Kites can also be used to carry lines across ravines.

Some kites can have colourful ribbon or fuzzy streamer tails of different colours along the tail length. A swivel helps them spin around. You can also have different coloured diamond or circle pieces along the tail, or a twenty foot hollow tube with different colours along its length, or stripes like a snake. You can even get forty -five foot tails which leave a trail in the sky. There are also wind tubes and windsocks and spinners which have tails attached.

Tails on planes are horizontal stabilizers giving yaw stability. They can be cruciform and mid mounted on the fin as in a Hawker sea hawk or a T tail, high mounted on the fin as in a Boeing 727.You can have two small tails to act as a single tail instead of one larger one as in a Havilland Vampire as its engine is in the centre. The exhaust is also shorter so that the tail pipe thrust is more effective. The tail bonanza plane 1947 was called the V-tail doctor killer. It cruised at 175 mph but often had structural failures in its wings and tails.

Many planes have tail designs which are often created by famous artists British airways examples have been included on Boeing 757s. Denmark had an abstract called 'wings' with shapes in bright colours to represent colonies of seagulls in flight The Chelsea rose was used for England, 'Dreaming' in Australia based on aboriginal design (Nalanji) containing fish and turtles, Japan has waves and cranes the waves for life and space and the cranes for the soul of Japanese beauty.

In world war two the person sitting at the tail end of the plane, a rear gunner, or the last ship in a flotilla was nicknamed' tail end-Charlie'.

Surfboards

The Pin Tail end is good for control in large waves. Its narrow width and pointed end allows the tail to sink in The round tail though has better versatility than the narrow pintail with a pointed end so one gets more lift and faster speeds. If the end is squarer you can get even more lift. If the tail is large and straight there is good stability and the corners help turns. If the tail is swallow tail there is more surface area for control in small waves and better control on turns.

Weather

In Victorian times one could buy a donkey or mule weather forecaster made of china or plaster. The following appearances of the tail would indicate the weather

Tail dry- fine weather

Tail wet -rain

Tail moves-windy

Tail cannot be seen-foggy

Tail is frozen-cold

Tail falls out-earthquake

A beaver's tail weather is a flow band which is broad and flat, orientated parallel to a pseudowarm front

Uranium

The word tail is used in the enrichment of uranium.
Uranium mill tailings are sandy process waste material
which contain radioactive decay products.

5 FOLK LAW SUPERSTITION AND PLANTS

Tails are often sold and used for spiritual purposes. Stroking the fur on a tail from a dead animal may produce physical attributes of that animal and its emotions For the Hindus the cows tail is the most sacred part of the animal.

The hairs on the tip of the cat's tail are often associated with strange, magical powers. Stepping on a cats tail could mean you will have bad luck and even remain an old maid and not get married. Burying parts or hairs of a cat will keep the cat at home. If a cat chases its tail then a storm may be approaching In Thailand if a small creature or insect lands in front of you and turns round to point its tail at you, you will be lucky and angels will look after you.

Plants linked to tails

Bunny or hare's tails grass (Lagurus ovatus)

This has spiky inflorescences that look like cotton tails of rabbits.

Cat tails plant (Typha latifolia)

This grows anywhere that is wet or marshy, especially around ponds. It has a fluffy seed head and is an aquatic plant.

Crested dog's-tail (Cynosurus cristatus)

Doggetail 13th /14th century plant. A perennial grass head of seed is flattened with bracts. Good for pasture.

Foxtail grass (Genus Alopecurus)

In western United States these have sharp awns with barbs that can dig into skin. It is a wild form of barley and examples are common worldwide.

Horsetails

In the carboniferous period huge horsetails were present. These like damp areas and are often associated with areas of silica or coal deposits. Its Latin name, Equisetum, comes from equus, a horse and seta meaning bristly.

Scorpion tail plant (Heliotropium angiospermum)

This is present in Guyana and also found in Europe. It is used as a tea and is supposed to help with stomach problems.

Tall tails grass (Pennisetum orientale)

This is a giant fountain looking grass with feathery flowers that cascade down

Catkins

These are often referred to as lambs' tails, the word originating from the Dutch meaning kitten. Lambs are also found in the fields where they are produced on the hazel trees so people have used the name lambs' tails as well

6 FICTIONAL CHARACTERS WITH TAILS

Animal mixtures with tails

There are many examples of animal and human mixtures. These include werewolves; the Egyptian god Bes had the back of a lion, also the sphinx. The minator had the head of a bull and the body of a human.

Mixtures of two animals include; Pegasus, a horse with the wings of a bird, Peryton, a stag with wings and various lions, unicorns and cats with wings, animals with half a fish and an elephant's head (Gaja Minah), half a fish and a horse (Hippocampus) and half a fish and a lion (Merlion).

Other examples of mixtures of animals with tails include Allocamelus- part donkey part camel; a cockatrice part reptile and a chicken, and Shug, part monkey part dog.

Nian was a beast with the head of a lion and body like a bull. At Chinese New Year it would eat children and livestock. Villagers put out food to stop him eating them. They knew he was afraid of the colour red, fire and noise. This is why on Chinese New Year they hang red scrolls on windows and doors and let off firecrackers.

The Aztecs of Mexico believed that Cipactli, the sea monster- part crocodile plus parts of a fish and toad helped create the cosmos. The gods wanted to start creation and were afraid the sea monster would stop them so they pulled the creature apart to form the heavens, the underworld and the earth. Its tail formed the underworld.

Examples with three animal parts include a Chimera consisting of the head and front legs of a lion, back legs of a goat and tail as the head of a snake. Simurgh was a griffin-like female creature of Persian mythology which had the head of a dog and the claws of a lion (although sometimes with a human face).

There are even some examples containing four animal parts. An Enfield had the head of a fox, forelegs and wings of an eagle, the body of a lion and tail of a wolf.

An example of five parts of an animal such as a Tarasque which had the head of a lion, legs of a bear, body of an ox, shell of a turtle and tail of a scorpion.

Fenghuang from China is one of the creatures that created the world. This time in one example the parts are all from birds It has the head of pheasant, body of a duck, tail of a peacock, legs of a crane, mouth of a parrot and wings of a swallow. It is said to have, even though multiformed, a beautiful song. Another example for Fenghuang includes different animals such as the forehead of a fowl, beak of a cock, neck of a snake, down of a duck, back of a tortoise. It has the marks of a dragon as it is female and paired with a dragon in marital harmony.

Costumes

Hugh Heffner's empire included bunny girls who had small bobtails on the back of them. If they left they were supposed to hand these in but many didn't. Mermaid tail fin costumes are sold which can be used in water. These can be various colours and are very popular at festivals and exhibitions. Other animal tails can be purchased which can be attached to people, from those of Mickey Mouse to thick dinosaur tails.

Devils and demons

The forked devil's tail is believed by some to be linked to the ends of a pitch fork which people used to ride just as witches rode broom sticks. It is also linked to arrows which, if covered in blood when hitting an enemy, showed they had a link with the devil. In Japanese mythology Demons with 1-10 tails are found in the world of Naruto. To remove them they had to be put inside new born babies but that would kill those who used this method.

Dragons and lions

Dragons may have their origins in China where they dug up huge bones which were from dinosaurs but attributed them to large creatures such as dragons.

They usually have   forked tail ends between which they poo. Poo is stored in their tails. But in some cases they are drawn as spade shaped.

In fable the lion was supposed to be able to wipe out his footsteps with his tail so that no-one could follow him.

Huldrefolk

These are found in Norwegian folk tales and are called the Hodden, invisible people. When a man marries a Huldre wife she becomes visible and can lose her tail if baptised. It is best not to mention her tail and just say what beautiful long hair she has running down her back to the floor.

Human tails

As a punishment for the murder of Thomas Becket in Canterbury Cathedral it is said that the men of Kent would be born with tails. Devon men also thought Cornish men had tails. In medieval time people from the continent were believed to have tails. In Japan eating parts of a merman can give immortality.

Merpeople

Merpeople are very common in Greek legends. Thought by some not to have a soul .In Slavic mythology they are seen as young, drowned women dragging young men down under the river to live with them. Mermaids usually are considered lucky. A mermaid has the top half of a woman and the bottom half of a fish with a tail. They are depicted as often upset, sitting on a rock in the sea and combing their long, golden hair. To see a mermaid can be a sign of approaching rough weather. Some are seen in medieval churches in Britain holding a starfish in their hands which represents a human soul which was lost by lusting for a mermaid. These sirens may lure men to their depths through singing. A Syrian goddess, Derceto, is depicted as a mermaid.

Mermen use a conch shell to make music and cause violent storms at sea. The Greek god Titan has a fish tail, as does Poseidon and Amphitrite. Gluacus in

Greek mythology fell into the sea where the gods made him a merman. In Trinidad and Tobago, sea-dwelling mermen could grant a wish, like a genii. The story of the Merrow of Ireland and Scotland involves a mermaid marrying a man. If her red cap is taken off or hidden she would shed her skin. Some Irish ancestors are believed to be merfolk. Often sea cows have been mistaken for merpeople in the past due to the fact that they carry their young in their arms like humans. . Many hoaxes exist where monkeys are attached to hind ends of a fish. Such a hoax was seen in the middle of the nineteenth century exhibited by the great showman PT Barnum and was a huge attraction at the time.

Snakes

The coach whip snake was said to squeeze its victim to death while lashing him. It would also make sure he died by putting his nits tail up the preys nostrils to stop him breathing.

In Norse mythology the world serpent is seen as biting its own tail while surrounding the world.

7 STORIES, POEMS, SONGS, JOKES AND GAMES ABOUT TAILS

Stories

Many books relating to animals use the word tails instead of tales in their title e.g. Dog days in Andalucía; tails from Spain by Jackie Todd, Edinburgh: Mainstream 2010.

Fox without a Tail one of Aesop's fables is about a
      fox who loses his tail in a trap and
tries to persuade other foxes that tails are not needed
      and are a problem. He is asked to turn
around and they realise he has lost his tail. The motto
      from this is do not listen to the advice of
him who seeks to lower you.

How Mr Rabbit Lost His Fine Bushy Tail is an
Uncle Remus tale from American Folk Law, Tales
sketches. It is the last series in 1881 compiled by Joel
Chandler Harris. It tells how Brer Fox went to the

creek and put his tail in the water and pulled out an armful of minnows. Brer rabbit went to the creek in cold weather and found a good spot. He put his tail in the water and drank a bottle of dram and waited. The river froze and he tried to pull out his tail and after a sudden jerk his tail came in two.

Humour of Dostoyevsky A writer's notebook by Somerset Maugham is about the humour of a bar-loafer who ties a kettle to a dog's tail.

How Mr Rabbit Lost His Fine Bushy Tail.is an Uncle Remus tale from American Folk Law, Tales sketches. It is the last series in 1881 compiled by Joel Chandler Harris.

Little Mermaid by Hans Anderson is a fairy tale written in 1836. It is a tale about a mermaid who saves a prince from a shipwrecked ship. She wants to become human and is in love with the prince so she gives up her voice to a sea witch so as to become human and be with her beautiful prince.
Unfortunately the prince has to marry a princess so

the sea witch keeps her voice and she believes that she will become foam on the sea. Hans Anderson puts in a happier ending in that she enters a spirit world and will go to heaven in three hundred years.

Teddy tails –a cartoon mouse in the Daily Mail newspaper 1915 was the first one to have speech bubbles.

Poems and Rhymes

Tail-rhyme often in English romances is where a pair of rhyming lines is followed by a single line of different length and this three line pattern is repeated to make a six line stanza Jack Harman has a poem.

Counting Piggy Tails is a bedtime lullaby. The first verse mentions tails; others include counting noses and baby pigs. With the mothers tail this reaches number eleven.

Elephant is from the bad child's book of beasts by Hilaire Belloc and refers to how people marvel at such a large beast such a little tail but a huge trunk in the front.

Little Bo Peep is a common children's nursery rhyme found in Gammer Curtins Garland or Nursery Parnassus produced in 1810(Peep means sleep in cockney slang).

Little Bo-Peep has lost her sheep,

And doesn't know where to find them;

Leave them alone, and they'll come home,

wagging their tails behind them

(Wagging may be replaced by dragging or bringing in some versions).

Three Blind Mice is an English nursery rhyme and relates to history. There may be an earlier version of 1609 which refers to tripe, instead of mice, but it is suggested that the farmer's wife was Queen Mary 1,

(Bloody Mary) who burnt three protestant bishops,

Ridley, Latimer and Cranmer, at stake for plotting

against her. The blind refers to them being

Protestants

Three blind mice, three blind mice,

See how they run, see how they run

They all run after the farmer's wife

Who cut off their tails with a carving knife

Did you ever see such a thing in your life?

As three blind mice?

What are little boys made of? is another popular

nursery rhyme by the English poet Robert Southey,

(1774-1843).

What are little boys made of?

What are little boys made of?

Snips and snails

And puppy-dogs 'tails

That's what little boys are made of

<u>Wife of Baths Prologue</u>, Canterbury Tales by
Geoffrey Chaucer

And after wyn on venus moste I thynke,

For al so siker as cold engendreth hayl,

A likerous mouth moste hn a likeroustayl

<u>Songs and music</u>

<u>Cotton Tail Jazz</u> by Duke Ellington in 1940 was
produced from an arrangement by George Gershwin.

<u>How much is that Doggie in the window?</u> by Bob
Merrill, 1952, is based on the song Oh where, Oh
where, has my little dog gone? from Carnival of
Venice

How much is that Doggie in the window?
The one with the waggly tail
How much is that Doggie in the window
I do hope that Doggies for sale

<u>Little Robin Redbreast</u> is an old English nursery rhyme and can have actions with it.

<u>Little Robin Redbreast</u> (Hold up thumb & little finger for head and tail)
Sat upon a rail;
(Place hand on arm)
Niddle noodle (or noble, naddle, noddle.)went his head,
(Wiggle thumb)
Wiggle waggle went his tail.

<u>Monkeys have no tails in Zamboanga.</u> This poem was sung by World War 2 pilots and John Wayne sang it in the film "Donovan's Reef" It refers to Zamboanga monkeys having no tails as they were bitten off by whales.

<u>Pussywillows</u> is a song by Gordon Lightfoot,
/Cat-tails lyrics is on the album. Did She Mention My Name in 1968 and Song book 1999. It contains the words Pussywillows cat-tails soft winds and roses which appear in summer.

<u>Put A Little Salt on the Bluebird's Tail</u> was by Wayne King and His Orchestra in the 1920s in his songs about animals.

<u>Raccoon got a bushy tail</u> was **an American Negro folk song** by SA Allen 1915

Opossum's tail is bare
Rabbit ain't got no tail at all
But jes'a bunch o'hair
Concludes white folks and black have no tails
But jes'a bunch o'hairs are about tails

<u>Top Hat, White Tie, & Tails</u> was a popular Irving Berlin song which became a film in 1935 starring Fred Astaire and Ginger Rogers

<u>'Tails and Trotters'</u> by Judy Goodenough Fox Chapel Pennsylvania 1982 where the chorus refers to pigs where all the sons and daughters are hocks, hams tails and trotters.

If everybody had a tail is from the Songs for Tomorrow Girl Guides Association 1984. It covers the many uses of tails and also what tails can do waving, wagging and even being chased.

<u>Other tails in music</u>

1940 **Cotton Tail** by Duke Ellington/Ben Webster. RCA

1949 **Blue Tail Fly** by Burl Ives. Decca records

1963 **Shake a Tail Feather** by The five DuTones. One-DERFUL

1965 **I've got a Tiger by the Tail** by Buck Owens. Capitol

1976 **A Trick of the Tail** by Genesis. Charisma records

1996 **The Half Tail** by Wolfstone. Green Linnet

2003 **Chasing your Tail** by Matt Savage. Savage

2003 **Devil by the Tail** by Overkill. Killbox 13 album

2007 **Both Ears and Tails** by Martin Carthy. Topic records

2008 **A Tail of Two Cities** by Gov't Mule. Evil Teen

2010 **Sting in the Tail** by scorpions Sony.NEWDoor/UME

Films and TV

Tail about tails is by Tish Rabe based on cat in the hat TV series.

An American Tail 1986 is a film about a young Russian mouse that emigrated to the US and gets separated from his family and tries to locate them. Animation Director Don Bluth.

Red tails is a film about American pilots in the Tuskegee Training Programme who were segregated to stay on the ground in World War 2 and then called to duty. Director Anthony Hemingway.

Jokes about tails

In many jokes about tails different animals can be substituted and still make the joke valid.

Q: What did the dog say when it got its tail caught in the door?

A: "It won't be long now!"

Q: Where does a dog go when it loses its tail?

A: To a re-tail shop.

Q: Mama is so fat she stepped on my cat's tail

A: Now I call him beaver!

Q: Why do dogs wag their tails?

A: Because no one else will do it for them!

Q: What has 2 arms, 2 wings, 2 tails, 3 heads, 3 bodies and 8 legs?

A: A man on a horse holding a chicken.

Q: Why is getting up at 3 o'clock in the morning like a pig's tail?

A: It's twirl.

Q: Why do mice have long tails?

A: Well, they'd look silly with long hair!

Q: What have 12 legs, six eyes, three tails and can't see?

A: Three blind mice!

Q: Why do pigs have curly tails?

A: Because they are born in the 'spring'.

A: Because they can't use straighteners.

Games with tails

Catch the Dragons Tail

This is a traditional Chinese game .Children line up with hands on the shoulders of the person in front so as to form a line. The front person is the dragon's head and tries to tag the last person in the line who is the tail so that they become the new dragons head. All the other players move back one place.

Capture creatures

A game from Olmega involves keeping order in the creature kingdom using their dinosaur tail which is covered in spikes of glass which explode on contact.

Pin the tail where one puts the correct tail on the animal is also another game.

Pin the tail on the donkey

The picture or drawing of a donkey without a tail is pinned up on a wall or door. Children have to pin the donkey's tail onto the donkey picture whilst blindfolded. The nearest to the correct position is the winner.

Sensei golden tail game (Wizards of the Coast Inc. Stephen Tappin)

This has a legendary character Fox Samurai. A counter placed on the target creature gains bushido 1 and becomes a samurai.

Tails

Tails originated is as an orange fox- like animal with two tails in the Sonic the hedgehog video games of 1955 from Sega Game Gear. He is Sonics' best friend and uses his tail to propel him into the air like a helicopter. Games have been developed for the Tails character.

Tiger Tag

There are various games for matching tails to the correct animal.

A variation of this is Tiger tag. Whoever it is wears the tiger mask and tail.

World Warcraft

Quest to get the wolves of Desolace and the Badlands wooden stick with soft bushy tail attached to it called savage fuzz tail.

8 TAILS FOUND IN QUOTES, SAYINGS AND WORDS

Examples of Quotes

Nine tailors make a man early (17th century)

 A gentleman should select his attire from a number of sources. This is also associated with bell ringing, the nine tailors being the nine knells traditionally rung for the death of a man.

Mid-17th century

It is idle to swallow the cow and choke on the tail when a serious matter is completed, waste of time arguing about a trifle.

Princess Anne- When I appear in public people expect me to neigh, grind my teeth, paw the ground and swish my tail-none of which is easy.

W H Auden-In times of joy, all of us wished we possessed a tail we could wag.

Buffalo Bill-I found Spotted Tail's lodge. He invited me to enter.

Lewis Carroll-How doth the little crocodile improve his shiny tail and pour the waters of the Nile on every golden scale.
The Cheshire cat vanished quite slowly, beginning with the end of his tail, and ending with the grin.

June Carter Cash -Every dog has his day, unless he loses his tail, then he has a weak-end.

Davy Crocket- Fame is like a shaved pig with a greased tail, and it is only after it has slipped through the hands of some thousands, that some fellow, by mere chance, holds on to it!

John Dryden-Roused by the lash of his own stubborn tail our lion now will foreign foes assail.

Albert Einstein-The wireless telegraph is not difficult to understand. The ordinary telegraph is

like a very long cat. You pull the tail in New York, and it meows in Los Angeles. The wireless is the same, only without the cat.

Clive James - Every sentence George Bush manages to utter scatters its component parts like pond water from a verb chasing its own tail.

T. E. Lawrence-To have news value is to have a tin can tied to one's tail.

Martin Luther Be thou comforted little dog, Thou too in Resurrection shall have a golden tail.

Abraham Lincoln-How many legs does a dog have if you call the tail a leg? Calling a tail a leg doesn't make it a leg.

Dian Ross- My family called me a wiggle tail because I was a little skinny, wiry kid full of energy.

Desmond Tutu-If you are neutral in situations of injustice, you have chosen the side of the oppressor. If an elephant has its foot on the tail of a mouse and you say you are neutral, the mouse will not appreciate your neutrality.

Arnold Topynbee-America is a large friendly dog in a small room. Every time it wags its tail it knocks over a chair.

Mark Twain-If you hold a cat by the tail you learn things you cannot learn any other way.

Some Sayings

As useful as a dog with two tails- to have something which is superfluous

Bit of tail –Irish slang for girl friend

Bright eyed and bushy tailed-full of energy, alert and eager

Can't make head nor tail of- unable to understand

Chasing tail-attack to the tail

Chasing one's own tail- rush around ineffectively

Better the head of a dog than the tail of a lion- better to be leading a small group than an individual in a larger group

Drag tail-leave, depart or move slowly

Freeze the tail off- to get very cold

Fuzzy tail- confused, indistinct

Get off my tail –stop following closely

Get one's tail in gear-get started, organised

Get ones tail somewhere fast- immediate action

Go chase your tail- go away

Happy as a dog with two tails-you look very happy

Has the world by the tail- with great influence, excessive self confidence

Have a tiger or bull by the tail- working on something powerful and dangerous

Heads or tails-two choices, obverse and reverse images on a coin

Hunk of a tail- slang someone to have intercourse

In two shakes of a lamb's tail- very quickly or short period

Nose to tail- too close e.g. cars

On tail- following someone closely

One tailed two tailed hypothesis- testing statistical significance relationships one or two directions

Piece of tail-sexual intercourse

Put salt on his tail-block or catch

Sting in the tail-some sort of rebuke or unexpected hurt at end of something done or said

To tail something in- insert end of brick etc.

Tails wagging the dog-less important things dominate the situation

To be with tail-French origin for coward for turning tail

To twist the lion's tail-provide resentment of the British lion's tail is British Empire

Turn tail and run-frightened turn around and run

Wet tail infection-in hamsters

With tail between their legs-a state of dejection

With ones tail up-in a confident or cheerful mood.

Work ones tail off-over work to exhaustion

Some common names of animals

Bartailed-Godwit, pheasant, hawk

Bartailed-Godwit, pheasant, hawk

Black tailed –Deer, prairie dog, godwit, tree creeper, bettong, possum, gull, shark

Brown tailed- Moth, mongoose, hawk, pencil fish, squirrel

Brush tailed- Bettong, phascogale, rat, kangaroo, golden possum, porcupine, rock wallaby

Cotton tailed-Rabbit, deer, tamarind

Fan tailed-pigeon, warbler, goldfish, raven, dove, guppy, water rabbit

Fat tailed – Dunnart, sheep, dwarf lemur, scorpions, gecko

Feather tailed-Glider, possum, catfish, centipede

Forktailed- Drongo, dragon caterpillar ,cat, petrel, gull, flycatcher, rainbow fish

Free tailed-Mexican bat

Long tailed-Jaeger, skua, spotted cat, duck, tit, field mouse, lizard, macaque

Pied-African wagtail

Pigtailed-Macaque

Pintail-Bahama, wrasse

Prehensile tailed-Porcupine, skink

Racquet tailed-Sulu green roller, greater dongo, buru, golden mantled, goldfinch, humming bird, kingfisher

Rat tailed-Maggot

Redtailed-Cockatoo hawk, phascogale, wambenger, shark, boa, catfish, black cockatoo, kite ,buzzard

Ringtail-Caotmundi, lemur, possum, gecko, common, hen harrier, cat, possum

Spotted tailed -Canadian tiger butterfly, quoll, fish, hawk, bass, salamander, cat

Tailorbird- South Asian warbler

Tailor fish-bluefish

Swallow tailed-Canadian tiger, gull, kite, hawk, hummingbird, moth, butterfly, bee eater

Wagtail-blue headed ,pied, grey, white, yellow

White cheeked-Pintailed bahama, turaco, gibbon, bulbil, spider monkey, tern

Whitetailed-Deer, jackrabbit, spider, sea eagle, bumblebee, hawk, mongoose

Yellow tailed-Lugworm, scorpions, black cockatoo, moth, wooly monkey, wagtail, bumblebee

Some words with tail in them with examples of meanings

Aventail-chain mail attached to base of helmet covering shoulders and neck

Bangtail-tail of horse or cow or a racehorse

Blacktail- handgun, animal

Brain tail- second brain in tail dinosaurs,

Bristletail-silverfish or firebrats

Broadtail-sheep or lamb with soft silky fur

Cattail-wetland plant, cigar shaped with furry seed heads

Cocktail-alcoholic drink with additional ingredients

Curtail-cut short or reduce

Dabble tail -slovenly woman who lets her gown get dirty in mud

Daggle tail-slovenly woman

Detail-particular parts

Dovetail-joints named as they resemble birds tail used in furniture even in Egyptian tombs

Ducktail-1950s hairstyle divided and meets at back

Entail-involve

Fantail-broad tail, like fan

Foxtail-bushy tail appearance like a fox

Hightail-file sharing

Horntail-wood wasp, hungry dragon in game

Horsetail-like tail of horse, primitive plant

Mocktails-alcohol free drink juice mixture

Oxtail-tail of ox use for soup, flavourings

Pigtail-single or double hair braid

Ponytail-hair gathered at back and tied or clipped

Rattail-single braid of hair in middle back of head

Redtail-reference to animals, wartime pilots

Retail-selling consumer goods or services

Ringtail-_reference to mammal's rings of colour on tails

Scaletail-African rodents with scaly tails e.g. squirrel

Scissortail-king birds with long forked tails

Shavetail- unbroken army mule whose tail was shaved 1840-1850

Shirttail-part of shirt hanging at back below waist

Short tails-criminal gang in New York who loved beer and lot of boat crimes

Swallowtail-V shaped form like tail of swallow can be seen also in healthy brains but absent with Parkinson's

Swordtail-fish with lancet at base tail fin

Tail- Hindmost part of an animal, appendage or long train or line

Person's buttocks

Part of the pancreas which organises enzyme activity

Street talk for vulva in Shakespeare's time

At the end of signatures, if high this is personal, the person wants to be noticed like waving

Writing the descender of a Q or the diagonal stroke of an R

In Italian Coda in music designates a passage that
brings a piece of a movement to the end
Refuse or dross remaining from a process of distilling
or milling
The short closing line of a stanza or verse
Bottom edge of a book
Lower part of coat worn by undertakers, at weddings,
ringmasters in circuses
Tailback-congested e.g. slow flowing traffic
Tailboard-tailgate
Tailbone-coccyx
Tail boom-main part of framework e.g. plane
Tailcoat-morning or evening coat with tails at the
back
Tail comb-comb with taping handle for styling
curling hair
Tail covert-small feathers in birds' tails covering the
base of large feathers
Tail dragger-aeroplane lands on its tail wheel with
nose up
Tailed-white tailed etc.
Tailender-last part of something
Tailfin-posterior part of fish

Tailgate-getting too close or hinged back of lorry

Tail guards -protects horses' tails if braided can be luminous in traffic

Tailer- hindmost part of animal, noose to hold fishes' tail

Tailing- residue of process e.g. iron ore, inferior flour, cutting stalks of vegetables or ends of fruit, part of a projecting wall

Taillamp or taillight-red light at end of vehicle or bike or even LEDS on horse's tail in traffic

Taille- the register of a tenor, Tax in France 1789, or juice from a second pressing.

Tailleur-suit, cross-legged

Tailfan-fan shape at back of bird or crustacean(telson)

Tail gas-not required for further processing

Tail hook-angling

Tail lift- on back of trailers

Taillike-like an animal's tail long and slender

Tailor- making fitted clothes

Tail male-limitation of succession for title or property to a male descendent

Tail of one's eye-outer corner of eye

Tail off-gradual reduction

Tailpiece- final end of something

Tailpipe-hole on rifle to hold ramrod or rear part of aeroplane, rear end section of an exhaust

Tailplane-horizontal aerofoil at aircraft tail

Tail race- fast river under dam

Tail rhyme-rhyme with couplets etc. that has additional short lines added

Tail rotor-auxiliary rotor on helicopter to counterbalance

Tailskid-supports tail of aeroplane when on ground

Tail slide-backward movement of aircraft

Tailspin-downward spiralling dive of an aircraft or loss of control

Tail stock-adjustable part of a lathe holding a spindle.

Tails and trotters-parts of a pig often eaten

Tail walk -to move over water by propulsion e.g. with tail

Tailwater-excess water, flowing water downstream from a dam or other structure good for fishing

Tail wheel -wheel supporting tail of an aircraft.

Tailwind- wind blowing in direction of vehicle

Tripletail-marine pelagic fish

Ventail-middle part of medieval helmet over nose and mouth flap of chain mail

Wagtail- bird that wags tail up and down when walking

Whiptail-animals with tail like a whip, computer data storage system

Whitetail-animals with white tail e.g. deer

Yellowtail tail-Australian wine, butterfly marine fish

ABOUT THE AUTHOR

Dr Mike Pearce is a scientist interested in behaviour. He also was a lecturer in human biology and health at a college in Canterbury, Kent.

www.ingramcontent.com/pod-product-compliance
Lightning Source LLC
Chambersburg PA
CBHW071214280526
45787CB00002B/683